Self Esteem for Teens

Six Proven Methods for Building Confidence and Achieving Success in Dating and Relationships

By

Maria van Noord

Table of Contents

Self Esteem For Teenagers

Chapter 1:

What is Self-Esteem?

Self-esteem, many times referred to as self-respect or self-worth, is a personality trait that plays a crucial role in the success of an individual. Another commonly accepted notion of self-esteem is that it is an individual's opinion about himself or herself. The level of your self-esteem depends on many factors and self-beliefs, such as:

- Do you believe you are doing a job worthy of your capabilities and qualifications? Do other people respect you for what you do?
- Do you think you are successful?
- What kind of self-image do you have?
- How do you feel about your weaknesses and strengths?
- Are you constantly comparing yourself with others and finding fault with yourself?
- What do you believe is your standing in your community and social circle?

In psychology, self-esteem is used to describe an individual's overall sense of personal value or self-worth. So, self-esteem can be defined as a measure of how much you like and appreciate yourself for what you are and do.

Self-esteem is a complex phenomenon because it is not a one-dimensional, easy-to-figure-out element of human life. It includes a multitude of beliefs and ideas including physical appearance, level of emotional quotient, behavioral tendencies, and more.

Like all things in the world, the self-esteem trait should also be balanced in an individual for optimal efficacy.

If a person has too little of this important personality characteristic, then he or she can feel disappointed and depressed. Such people will not even get into any venture in the first place because they lack self-belief and self-confidence - both of which are interminably intertwined with self-esteem.

Signs of low self-esteem include a lack of confidence, inability to articulate your needs and desires, focusing excessively on your weaknesses, feelings of anxiety, shame, depression, and fear of failure. Low self-esteem fuels your negative thoughts, weakens your resolve and makes you believe that you are how others perceive you.

On the other hand, people with excessive self-esteem could end up having a narcissistic personality; which is again self-destructive, frequently damages personal and professional relationships irrevocably, and is quite easily one of the most off-putting traits in a person.

Healthy self-esteem is crucial for success, happiness, contentment, and staying motivated to meet and overcome the challenges you encounter in your life. Here are some signs of healthy self-esteem: confidence, the ability to refuse or say no, a positive outlook, the ability to identify and accept strengths and weaknesses, not being unduly impacted by negative experiences, and the ability to articulate your needs and desires.

Is self-esteem nature or nurture? While there is a biological and genetic connection to our behavior and that of our parents and grandparents, genetics and biology do not decide our destiny and cannot really interfere with what we want to become. Moreover, none of us are really born with low self-esteem.

Look at babies from different cultural, racial, and economic backgrounds, and you can see there is hardly any difference in the way they behave. They smile when they are comfortable, fed, and happy. They cry if they are hungry, sleepy, or uncomfortable. No other emotion is really visible in a child.
As babies grow and interact with people around them and get influenced by what they see, hear, and sense, new emotions come to the fore and self-esteem along with its myriad layers of self-confidence, assertiveness, and more also makes an appearance. Low self-esteem is invariably a result of external circumstances, and our interactions with and reactions and responses from other people.

Challenges for Modern-Day Teenagers

Teenage years or the time of adolescence is, perhaps, one of the most sensitive and difficult phases of your life. Multiple emotional and physical changes are taking place in your body and minds, and many of these changes are beyond your control.

As a teenager, you face various challenges including bullying, tremendous academic pressure, body image issues, relationship woes, addictions of different types such as drugs, TV and electronic devices, and, of course, the wrath of the raging hormones. All these factors drive your anxiety and stress to unhealthy levels.

Signs of low self-esteem in teenagers are numerous including poor academic performance, being a victim of or participating in bullying, unprepared and early sexual activity resulting in frequent teen pregnancies, dropping out of school, criminal behavior, alcohol and drug abuse, and disordered eating.

Likely Causes for Low Self-Esteem in Teenagers

So, if we are not born with low self-esteem what can be the likely causes for developing this? Self-esteem at a teenage level comes from various sources including your parents, peers, and teachers. The people you interact with on a daily basis can affect your opinion about yourself.

Additionally, the thoughts that you focus on also plays an important role in either building up or bringing down your self-esteem. Let us look at some of the reasons for low self-esteem among teenagers a bit in detail so that you can identify your own triggers, and find ways to overcome these challenges:

Negligent or uninvolved parents - When your parents or guardians focus on your good traits, you feel good about yourself, and if they focus excessively on your bad qualities showing little or no patience to give you time to get better, then your self-esteem could be hit badly.

Negative peers – Just like parents, if you are surrounded by peers and friends who focus on the bad excessively then your self-esteem will take a beating. Choosing your social group plays an important role in the way your self-esteem takes shape.

Trauma – Sexual, emotional, physical, or a combination of these kinds of abuses takes a big toll on self-esteem, and if left untreated can create bigger psychotic problems.

Body image – How you perceive your body affects your self-esteem. Do you think you are fat, ugly, have horrible freckles, are too short, too dark, etc.? Then you have a problem with self-esteem because body image plays a significant role in the self-esteem of teenagers.

Unrealistic expectations – Some teenagers expect excessive amounts from themselves. They want to do well in academics, in sports, be popular in their social circles, and more. These unrealistic expectations can make you feel that you are not able to meet your desires and goals which, in turn, results in low self-esteem.

Self-Esteem Self-Discovery Quiz
Answer the following questions to identify your self-esteem levels. Then you can work on filling the gaps:
1. Do you think that people find you boring to talk to?
2. Do you believe that you are always messing things up?
3. Do you think that no-one will notice if you are missing from a party or social gathering?
4. Do you feel that you are constantly letting down people who

love and trust you and that you are not good enough for them?

5. Do you think that you can never achieve anything worthwhile?
6. Do you think you are a failure?
7. Do you think that people will respect and love you only if you are great-looking or successful?
8. Do you think you have to be as good as other people to be included in a social group?
9. Do you think you can never be as skilled as you should be?
10. Do you believe you don't deserve to be loved?

The answers to the above questions are not always a perfect 'yes' or a perfect 'no.' Reflect on the questions for a while. Try to recall events in your life that you can relate to the questions. Use the experiences from these past events to answer the questions. You will be able to discern whether you are happy or unhappy with your level of self-esteem, and what areas you need to work on.

Chapter 2:

The Components of Building Self-Esteem

As a teenager undergoing stresses and anxieties, healthy self-esteem will not only help you do well in school and be a stellar performer among your peers and friends but will also be the cornerstone of your adult life. As you step out alone into the big wide world, you will find the courage and strength needed to stave off and overcome challenges thrown at you and emerge strong, happy, and contented with your efforts in particular and your life in general.

Nathaniel Branden, a qualified psychotherapist, was one of the most influential writers on the subject of self-esteem. In his book 'The Six Pillars of Self-Esteem,' Nathaniel Branden has spoken about the six crucial components of self-esteem which include:
1. Living consciously
2. Self-acceptance
3. Self-responsibility
4. Self-assertiveness

5. Purposeful living
6. Personal integrity
7. Let us look at each of these six components in a bit of detail.

The Practice of Living Consciously

As a teenager, you might not yet have been introduced to the concept of conscious living. You get up each morning, get ready, go to school, attend classes, do your assignments, prepare for tests, go out with friends, have relationships, and do everything else that a growing adolescent will do without giving much thought to each of these activities. You live like a robot but breathe like a human being.

Now, living consciously would mean being aware of your feelings, emotions, and sensations as you do each of these activities. So when you wake up each morning, pause for a while, and gather your thoughts. What are you thinking? Are you looking forward to the day? What is it that you are looking forward to? Is it a particular class or meeting up with your partner, or something else?

Be aware of your feelings when you wake up. Similarly, when attending a class, observe your classmates and observe your teacher's voice, his or her words and engage in the class, all the while being aware of how you are behaving and feeling. Be conscious of every activity you indulge in during the day.

Without self-awareness or conscious thought, we are frequently giving in to our emotions instead of thinking calmly and objectively about a given situation. When we make an effort to be self-aware and do everything consciously, we will identify those situations when our emotions are taking over our minds and compelling us to react in a particular way.

When you can identify such situations, you can make the necessary corrections and behave and respond in a better way than before. Living consciously is the first step to becoming self-aware which, in turn, helps you improve yourself and work constructively to build your self-esteem.

The Practice of Self-Acceptance

Nathaniel Branden says that 'self-esteem is what we feel and self-acceptance is what we do!' Self-acceptance is accepting yourself the way you are, without a feeling of like or dislike. It is simply, "This is who I am." Let me illustrate with an example. Suppose you are a great football player, and you have won your team many matches. So, you are confident of this skill and you are full of self-esteem on the football field.

Now, shift to the classroom. Your level of academic skill may not be as good as the toppers in the class. Does that mean you should have low self-esteem in class? Not really. The trick is in self-acceptance. Identifying and accepting your strengths and weaknesses without being judgmental is the second most important component of self-esteem.

Accepting your weakness or strength has nothing to do with whether you like it or not. It is simply accepting yourself for what and who you are. Self-acceptance only means to allow yourself to be who you are, without having to seek approval from other people. At this point in time, you are fine with who you are. Acceptance of a weakness does not in any way mean that you are stuck there. In fact, it is the first step to making improvements so that you can overcome that particular weakness.

Interestingly, this self-acceptance includes the acceptance of your resistance to accepting yourself the way you are, if such a situation exists in your life! So, importantly, remember that it is perfectly alright to be who you are at the moment. The future can always be changed for the better. But, right now, don't regret being that person and having a particular personality that combines some strong and some weak traits. Self-acceptance is the reflection of your determination to improve yourself.

The Practice of Self-Responsibility

After self-awareness and self-acceptance are done with, you have to move on to the third important component of self-esteem: self-responsibility. If you continue to see yourself as a victim, it means you are looking for the person or situation victimizing you to change so that you can improve. That is never going to happen because being a victim means you are not in control because the seeming victimizer is holding control of your life. Consequently, your self-esteem is never going to improve.

Taking responsibility for yourself is taking back control of your life. Nobody can take responsibility for our happiness and fulfillment but ourselves. You might get help from people who love and care for you, but your ultimate ability to achieve a satisfying level of self-fulfillment will come only when you take responsibility for everything in your life.

For example, if the top person in your class is not helping you with a particularly difficult chapter, don't blame him. Simply find another source which can help you. It could be your teacher, the internet, another topper, or someone else in a different class. You have to take responsibility that you need help in that chapter and find ways to learn and master it. Instead if you sit doing nothing except wallowing in self-pity that you are not getting help, this will not raise your self-esteem.

In fact, remember one little thing. If someone is not willing to help you, he or she is truly contributing to your success because now you will be compelled to rely on yourself to do what you thought would be done by someone else. When you are driven to do something you will learn to do it well, and your self-esteem will automatically get a shot in the arm. The person who refuses to help you is facilitating the practice of self-responsibility.

No one can make you happy. If you are waiting for that perfect relationship to make you happy, then you'll wait forever because no perfect person will be coming to save your life. Stop waiting for help; take responsibility for yourself and get to work.

Also, you can be and are responsible only for the things that you can control. For example, suppose you have worked hard, did a test and scored better than your previous time. But the topper has still managed to do better than you. Take responsibility for your work and your efforts which helped you get better grades than you did before. You cannot take responsibility for what the topper did, and feel bad that you could not beat him. That is not in your control.

Take cognizance of the things that you can control and those that you cannot control. Typically, this part of learning about self-responsibility can also be included in the living consciously component of self-esteem. As you live consciously, you will be able to differentiate and accept things that you can and cannot control.

The Practice of Self-Assertiveness

Assertiveness is a term that is referred to a personality trait that is useful at getting you what you want. It is typically associated with getting something extra for yourself and your team. An assertive person is one who holds an advantageous position at a negotiation table over someone whose assertiveness qualities are found wanting.

Self-assertiveness is a little deeper than this, and means you have to learn to acknowledge and honor your needs and desires. Living and expressing your life the way you want to is self-assertiveness.

You start the journey of building esteem by first learning to become self-aware through conscious living, then accepting yourself for who you are and the way you are followed by taking responsibility for your own life's fulfillment and happiness.

Now you come to a stage when you learn to identify and honor your needs and values. Another commonly associated term for self-assertiveness is authenticity, which means being true to yourself. However, being self-assertive, in addition to being honest about your wants, needs, and desires to yourself, also means articulating these elements well so that you reflect your original inner personality to the outside world.

Self-assertiveness means being honest about speaking your

mind, even if it means being unpopular with people. You must be ready to face aversion if you are genuinely self-assertive. Self-assertiveness, therefore, translates to living to fulfill your expectations in life and not other people's expectations.

Self-assertiveness is not easy to perfect. As you lead your life with increasing consciousness, you will notice that more often than not it is easier to give in and surrender to people's expectations and do their bidding than it is to assert yourself and face unpopularity and even derision.

A classic example of self-assertiveness as a teenager; you are under a lot of peer pressure to go to a party where drugs and booze are bound to flow. You know that you need to complete that important grade-affecting math assignment that's due in a couple of days. You are sure you need to assert yourself and tell your friends you are going to miss this party. However, fearing ridicule from your friends it is typically easier to give in to their pressure than stand your ground and miss the party so that you can complete the assignment.

Such a situation is familiar to many teenagers, right?

The Practice of Living with Purpose

The most successful people in the world are those who had a clear purpose even as young teenagers. Here are a few classic examples:
- Bill Gates was falling in love with computers as a teenager.
- By the time Warren Buffet was 16, he was earning a lot of

money for himself and learning the ways of multiplying his money.

- Oprah Winfrey joined her school's debate team knowing for sure she wanted to talk her way through life, and by the time she was 16 she had landed a job as a broadcaster at WVOL, a local radio station in Nashville, where she was going to school.

When you have set a purpose for your life early on, you will have a deliberate direction. Knowing and visualizing your goal will keep you productive and prevent you from straying from your chosen path. When you advance on your path with little or no intention to waver from it, that act itself can be a huge contributor to your self-esteem.

Choosing a goal should be one that is for yourself alone. Of course, taking advice from family and well-wishers is great. But don't allow your life's purpose to be dictated by others' opinions and dreams. Additionally, setting a goal should be specific, including timelines, a list of activities you will indulge in to achieve your goal, and how you will measure your advancements. When you make your progress measurable, you will be to track results and be aware of whether you are on the right path or if you need to make adjustments.

Having a purpose in life facilitates self-discipline driven by the self-monitoring mechanism, using which we can drive and adjust ourselves continuously. Keeping a goal and moving towards it is a great proof that we can rely on ourselves and our capabilities.

The Practice of Personal Integrity

With the above five points, you have taken care of the majority of the elements needed for improved self-esteem. You are working towards your purpose and goal of life. Now you have to ensure that your actions and behaviors are in line with your values. The more your life is aligned with your own values, the more your self-esteem will rise because you will have the confidence that you are sufficiently well-equipped to manage your life and life goals on your own. You have the ability to face and overcome challenges.

Of course, you will face a lot of situations where the 'unpopularity' tag might follow you around.

For example, take the illustration of having to skip that party to complete your assignment. This would typically be based on your life goal of finishing college with flying colors so that your chances for success in the outside world are high. Your popularity among your peers took a dip. But you stayed on course.

The grades at the end of the term will substantiate your stand and personal integrity, and your self-esteem will definitely go up a few notches. The 'unpopularity' tag may not go away but you will not be bothered with it anymore because you have chosen to align your path to your values and chosen to stay on this path, despite difficulties.

Straying from your path might give you a temporary good feeling because you feel accepted by your friends. But, more importantly, straying from your chosen path is also a reflection of self-rejection which, in turn, will lead to low self-esteem.

Ask yourself who or what is standing in the way of your personal integrity. It is imperative to identify these major obstacles to improving self-esteem and continuously work on them until you live your life happily and on your own terms.

In addition to the above six components of self-esteem, Nathaniel Branden says that self-esteem has two parts: one part is that of self-efficacy which is the confidence you have in your skills to manage certain situations, and the second part is self-respect which means you believe you are worthy of joy and happiness. He further adds that it is better to be confident in your ability to learn and expand your knowledge rather than in your current level of skills and knowledge.

Self-esteem is not about being perfect. It is the acceptance of who we are in any given situation, including those that remind us of our weaknesses and inabilities. The best way to enhance self-esteem is to be open to continuous learning. The more you learn, the better you get. To be in a state of constant learning, you have to always move out of your comfort zone. Discomfort is the best teacher because it drives our body and mind to find ways to get comfortable, resulting in increased learning.

It is not just facing discomfort when it comes to your self-esteem. You must seek discomfort so that your learning curve is always on the rise. The outcome of seeking discomfort and enhancing learning is high self-esteem.

The best part of building self-esteem is the fact that the power for it lies in your hands alone. You don't need to depend on anyone or anything outside of yourself to love, respect, and have a worthy image of yourself. Take this quiz and see where you

17

stand currently when it comes to self-esteem, then use this to help you identify loopholes and work to fill up the gaps.

Self-Assessment Questions for Living Consciously

These are NLP (Neuro-Linguistic Programming) based self-awareness questions that will help you understand your current status of living consciously:

1) Do you see images in your mind?

a) I do not see images or pictures in my mind or I am only minimally aware of them.

b) Sometimes, I see images in my mind. But I don't know that I can control them.

c) I can see images in my mind vividly, and can work with and control them by altering the size, shape, color, etc.

2) Do you hear your inner sounds clearly?

a) I do not hear inner sounds clearly at all. In fact remembering music, conversation details, etc. are difficult for me.

b) I can hear inner sounds, and remembering music is ok. However, I don't know if I can control them or know how to connect with them.

c) I am very aware of the inner sounds playing in my head, and can control them by adjusting their volume, altering their sound, tone, pitch, location, etc.

3) How deeply do you connect with your feelings?

a) Not much at all. I'm more of a head person.

b) Sometimes I am aware of my emotions. But I don't know how to control them.

c) I am very much in touch with my feelings. I can differentiate between them, label them, convert negative to positive and vice versa, etc.

4) What triggers set off reactions from you?

a) I have no idea what sets me off; when I feel bad I simply react.

b) I do have triggers, and if I think deeply enough I could come up with a couple of them. But I don't think proactively about these triggers, and I don't know what to do with them.

c) I know exactly which stimulus sparks me off. I am aware when I'm not reacting in a nice way. I can often identify the trigger that makes me do so.

5) Do you know your limitations? Are you aware of the things you are good at and those that are you are not good at?

6) Do you know your personal beliefs and values? Do you know your capabilities?

7) Do you know what you value the most in your life?

8) What are your inner conflicts?

9) What kind of parental impact have you had on your life? How do your interactions with them affect you?

10) What about your peers and partners? How do they impact your life?

Self-Assessment Questions for Self-Acceptance

1) Do you keep comparing your capabilities with those of other people to feel worthy?

2) Do you set goals based on what others want?

3) Do you frequently attempt to categorize yourself as good, bad, average, etc.?

4) Do you feel pained, angry, hurt or resentful if you or your work is criticized?

5) Do you focus excessively on the weaknesses which make you dislike your personality?

Self-Assessment Questions for Self-Responsibility

1) Do you believe that your actions and behaviors are reflective

of how you want to lead your life?

2) Do you think that your reactions are your responsibility, irrespective of what caused the reactions?

3) Do you take responsibility for your physical health and ensure you take your dose of exercise, good nutrition, and restful sleep?

4) Do you believe that you are responsible for your happiness?

5) Do you think your values and principles of life should be your choice and not those of your parents, peers, friends, etc.?

6) Do you make the effort to seek help when you need it?

Self-Assessment Questions for Self-Assertiveness

1) Do you take pains to do what you believe in, even if it means being unpopular with people who care about you and love you?

2) Do you make efforts to live your life based on your values and principles?

3) Do you believe that even if you need to be present in a place that you don't like, how you choose to spend quality time there is up to you?

Self-Assessment Questions for Purposeful Living

1) Where do you see yourself when you are twenty years old; in college or somewhere else?

2) Have you set clear, specific, timebound, and measurable goals for yourself?

3) Do you keep track of your progress?

4) What are the triggers that drive you away from your goals? What helps you stay on course?

Self-Assessment Questions for Personal Integrity

1) How often do you lie to your parents, teachers, and peers?

2) Do you think you will accept a mistake you make if you think there is an easy way to get away with it?

3) Do you believe you lead a life that is aligned with your goals and purposes?

Chapter 3:

Habits and How to Use Them for the

Good

Habits are behaviors or rituals that we perform automatically without thinking. Human beings are creatures of habit, and we continue to activate new habits every day. Typically, habits can be divided into three categories:

1. Habits we don't notice – such as brushing our teeth, tying our shoelaces, etc.
2. Good habits – like going for your morning run every day, sleeping and waking up on time each day.
3. Bad habits – like smoking, procrastinating, addictions to video games, etc.

All of us want to cultivate good habits and get rid of bad habits. Habits are so complex that understanding and changing them by diagnosing each of them separately can be quite a challenge. Moreover, each bad habit is unique and calls for a different technique in order to be broken. For example, breaking the bad habit of smoking requires a different tactic from breaking the bad habit of excessive eating.

Charles Duhigg, in his book 'The Power of Habit,' discussed the habit loop through which he attempts to show readers that by understanding how habits work, it is possible to change any bad, unproductive habit into a useful and productive one. He speaks of a simple neurological loop that can cover any habit you have, and then shows you how to use effective methods to alter or eliminate the habit suitably.

The neurological loop of any habit consists of:
- The Cue
- The Routine
- The Reward

If you can identify the component loops of your bad habits, you can find ways to replace bad habits with good ones.

The Cue

A cue is typically a trigger that puts your brain into an automatic mode and drives it to follow a habit without thinking. Here are some types of cues that trigger a habit:

Time – This is the most common trigger of habits. Regular morning habits are a classic example. You wake up, walk into the bathroom, brush your teeth, take a shower, get dressed, have breakfast or a cup of coffee, and get to class or lab or any other college-related activity.

Identify the cue for the bad habit. Now, look at your bad habit and pay attention to see if there is a specific time that triggers it. For example, do you walk to your college cafeteria for a plate of fries at around 11 in the morning or 3 in the afternoon? If yes, then take stock of your feelings during those times. Is it hunger or boredom or loneliness that makes you do that?

Use this cue to replace the bad habit with a good one. So, at around the time when the bad habit kicks off, place reminders to focus on something productive. For example, keep your books close to you so that you can use that time cue to start reading or writing your assignment. If it is hunger, then make sure you have some healthy snack in your bag to dig into.

Location – Another powerful cue to set off habits is your location. For example, how many times have you walked into the kitchen to reach into a jar of cookies and eaten a couple of them without thinking? Now to change the habit to something good, keep away cookies so that you can't reach or see them and so will not get a chance to eat them. Additionally you can replace the cookie jar with a bowl of fruit so that you change your habit of eating healthy food.

Preceding events – A great example of this is when your phone rings. After you answer your call, invariably your brain is tuned to check out your social media notifications. Now, you can use such preceding event illustrations to set up good habits.

For instance, you can create a habit of meditating for a couple of minutes while you are getting your morning coffee or breakfast. Or you could make a note of two things that happened during the day that you are grateful for when you sit down for your evening meal, or just before retiring to bed.

Emotional status – Have you reached for the ice-cream whenever you felt depressed? Or have you gone on a shopping spree when you are angry or upset? The emotional states of anger or sadness are perfect cues to set off bad habits.

Identifying an emotional state to start off a good habit is a much bigger challenge than using cues like time, location, etc. Emotions can unwittingly overpower us. So it might make sense, at least initially, to only prevent yourself from behaving rashly instead of trying to replace your bad habit.

Recognizing the emotional status cues and simply paying attention mindfully to the emotion can help to prevent you from moving into the routine part of the habit. You could perform basic breathing exercises during times of emotional stress, and see how much difference that makes.

Other people – The people around you have a big impact on the habits that you inculcate. Studies have proven that if you are surrounded by obese friends, the chances of you becoming obese are higher than if you are surrounded by fit and healthy people.

So, the most effective way to inculcate and build good habits is to surround yourself by friends who have good habits. If you need to go to the gym each morning, make friends with someone who never misses his or her gym time. If you wish to eat healthily, make friends with people who count calories during their meals. If you wish to improve in your academics, make friends with the toppers and the studious people in your class.

If you want to break the habit of smoking, stay away from friends who smoke. If you want to quit excessive partying, stay away from friends who host and attend too many parties.

The Routine

The routine is the physical, emotional or mental action that you take after your brain receives the cue. In the examples stated above, the routine was in the form of:

- Walking into the college cafeteria at 11 in the morning and/or 3 in the afternoon
- Putting your hand into the jar of cookies when you walk into the kitchen
- Looking at social media notifications when you receive a call
- Binge-eating or going out shopping when depressed
- You also looked at how you can use the cues of time, location, preceding events, and emotional status to convert your bad-habit routines into good-habit routines such as:
- Keeping books with you so that you can study instead of walking to the cafeteria
- Replacing the jar of cookies with a bowl of fruit
- Using preceding events to remind you to meditate or write thank-you notes
- Meditating during bouts of high emotion instead of indulging in retail therapy or binge-eating

The Reward

The reward is that ultimate prize or end result of the habit which helps your brain to determine whether this particular loop is worth the effort of keeping in and recalling from memory. The reward is typically stored as a craving in your brain which drives the habit loop. In the above examples, rewards are typically the joy of eating that plate of fries or cookies or reading up interesting but useless gossip on social media or the act of retail therapy.

To change your habits, you can experiment with rewards instead of depending only on what the bad habits promise you. For example instead of walking to the college cafeteria, why don't you walk to the college library? If meeting with friends is the reward for the walk to the cafeteria, why don't you fix a different place for that? Convert the joy of eating a cookie into the joy of drinking a glass of fresh juice.

The way to build healthy habits and get rid of bad habits is to recognize the habit loop and get your brain to alter the cues, routines, and rewards suitably.

Self-Assessment of Bad Habits
Look at the following common bad habits among teenagers, and ask yourself if you are a victim of any of them:
- Biting fingernails
- Chewing gum
- Complaining
- Procrastinating
- Drinking excessively
- Smoking cigarettes or pot
- Excessive junk food
- Lack of exercising
- Spending too much time on the internet
- Coming late
- Playing online games or gambling
- Spending too much money
- Using bad words

- Gossiping
- Not showing gratitude
- Shopping when you're hungry
- Not saving money
- Dressing shabbily
- Binge-watching
- Breaking relationships without letting your partner know; ghosting relationships
- Leaving your dishes in the sink thinking your parents will handle them
- Telling white lies; a classic example of saying you turned in your assignment without actually having done so
- Not planning your study

Some of these habits might appear innocuous. But the unfortunate thing about bad habits picked up during your teenage years is that they invariably last your entire lifetime. And, fortunately, good habits picked up during your teenage years also last your entire lifetime. Therefore it makes a lot of sense to spend time and energy to break bad habits and build good ones. Moreover, bad habits during teenage years will not have typically reached the irreversible stage making it relatively easy to get rid of them.

Step-by-Step Guide to Starting Good Habits
Step 1 - Identify the habit you want to start. Define the cue that will trigger the start of your routine. At what time is the cue most likely to be triggered (time)? Where will you be when the cue is triggered (location)? What will be the preceding event? What will be your emotional status?
Step 2 - Define the rewards when the routine is done. Do you crave this reward? How do you feel when you get the reward?

Step 3 - Define the routine.

Step 4 – Put all these elements together and write the new habit down. Make sticky notes of the new habits and put them up at unmissable places so that your memory is triggered at the right times and in the right locations.

Here is a simple example: When I see (preceding event) my toothbrush at night, I will brush (routine) my teeth for that lovely, clean, and fresh feeling in my mouth (reward).

Step-by-Step Guide to Breaking Bad Habits

Step 1 – Identify the bad habit you want to break. What is the cue for it? What time? Where? Who are the people around you? What are the preceding events? What is your emotional status?

Step 2 – Define the reward or the craving the bad habit is satisfying. Experiment with other rewards that give similar satisfaction. You have to keep experimenting with your rewards until you find the ones that make the craving of the bad habit go away.

Step 3 – Now, define the routine and put the entire thing together. Make sticky notes and place reminders all over to ensure you don't fall for the wrong cues and experiment with new rewards.

Chapter 4:

Practical Examples

This chapter is dedicated to giving you practical examples of how you can build self-esteem by building on the six components discussed in Chapter 2.

The Practice of Living Consciously

NLP techniques

NLP or Neuro Linguistic Programming helps you 'upgrade your mind.' NLP techniques help with improving your intelligence, memory, mindset, and communication skills by aligning your conscious mind with your unconscious mind. NLP stands for:

- Neuro – pertains to the brain's communication tools; the nerves and the neurons
- Linguistic – pertains to the language of the mind
- Programming – refers to setting something to work in a particular way.

Here are some NLP techniques to help you live your life with improved consciousness:

Pay attention to your thoughts – Our unconscious minds are affected by what we think about the most. For example, if your thoughts are that you are not going to pass the upcoming school test then your conscious mind and your body are going to resist your attempts to prepare for the test.

Instead, if your thoughts are 'I am going to work hard to pass the school test with flying colors,' then your body and your conscious mind will be aligned with these positive thoughts and you will find it easy to focus on studying hard which, in turn, will definitely help you clear your test well.

Prayers – Prayers are nothing but wishes or hopes that some things will happen the way you want them to. Prayers give you a sense of faith that your wish or hope will come true.

For example, if you repeatedly pray that you get selected for your school's basketball team then your conscious mind adopts it and passes it on to the subconscious mind, and drives your entire bring to believing and accepting the importance of this prayer. Moreover this prayer gives you faith that your expectations will come true, and faith will drive you to work hard to achieve your dreams.

Affirmations

Use affirmations to live consciously. Create positive feelings by using affirmations. Here are some affirmations you can use:

- I deserve to be loved
- I have the power to bring about positive changes in my life
- I am strong enough to make my own decisions
- I have the power to be happy irrespective of external circumstances

Visualization

Visualization helps to direct your mind and body towards the path of your goal without being negatively impacted by the outside world. A classic example of a highly successful person who used their visualization to high levels of success is Nikola Tesla, a man who gave us the AC induction motor, wireless communication, and over 700 patented inventions, many of which are still in use today. Apparently he would build the device in his imagination first, and only then make it a tangible product.

Even though you may think you are not anywhere near Tesla's superhuman levels, his life is an example of the power of visualization that each of us is endowed with. Use it effectively to live consciously. Visualize victories and happy days. Work towards crystallizing those mind visuals.

Meditation

Meditate regularly to connect with your thoughts and emotions. This will help you become more conscious of these elements in your life, and you will be able to discern between good and bad thoughts. For example, start your morning with a 10-minute meditation during which time you can acutely visualize how you want your day to unfold. Make sure you focus on the positives so that you start your day on a positive note which empowers your body and mind to be prepared to take on the challenges of the day.

Maintaining a Diary

Maintaining a diary which you update regularly helps you in many ways:
First, it makes you more aware of what has happened during the

day. For example, suppose a test score was announced in school and your scores were really good. However you did not have time to respond emotionally because the teacher for the next subject walked into class, and you got sucked into the day's activities.

When you sit down to update your diary at the end of the day, you will get the required time to truly appreciate your hard work which paid off by getting you great scores. You become more acutely aware of the happiness of having worked hard for which you got suitably rewarded, thereby improving your connections with your emotions and feelings.

Second, it gives you reasons to feel gratitude. As you pass through your day in a rush, you will not find enough time to think deeply about the many good things that happened to you during the day. When you sit down to make entries in your diary at the end of each day, you will get sufficient time to be grateful for all the good things of the day.

Third, you will find the power to look at the negative things of the day without the attached emotion, which will help you learn important lessons for the future.

The Practice of Self-Acceptance

NLP Techniques

Anchoring for self-acceptance – Anchoring is an NLP technique that allows you to anchor feelings of positivity through the use of a physical sensation.

For example, remember that feeling of happiness you had when you led your school team to victory in the interschool basketball match. Recall the ecstatic feelings associated with that event, and simultaneously rub your index finger and thumb together or touch your right ear or perform any other convenient action. Keep repeating the chosen action each time you recall those great times. This is the anchoring process.

During moments of self-doubt, perform the physical action connected to those happy thoughts. This will help you to overcome self-doubts and accept yourself as you are.

Affirmations
If you don't love and accept yourself first, the chances of others accepting and loving you are low. Self-love and self-acceptance are primary elements of self-esteem. Use affirmations for self-acceptance:

- I am worthy of love, joy, and happiness
- I approve of myself
- I am complete by myself and do not need anything more to complete me
- My life is a gift to me. I will use it with exuberance and confidence
- I will surround myself only with positivity

Visualization
Visualizations can help in building self-acceptance and self-love. Always visualize yourself as being happy and joyful. Imagining yourself as a happy-go-lucky and fun-loving person will make your brain think it to be true, and will create physical impulses and reactions that are aligned with this happy mood.

For example, it is common for a smile to come on your face

when you visualize something pleasant. Haven't you come across a situation where a friend has asked you why you are smiling? And only then it has struck you that you have a smile on your face. That is the power of visualization. You visualize something nice, and it gets reflected in your body. Similarly, when you visualize something bad either tears well up or a frown automatically forms on your face.

Self-love through visualization will, therefore, be reflected in your body language. When you love yourself and accept your strengths and weaknesses with humility, your level of confidence takes a boost and it will be reflected in the spring of your step or that confident smile.

Meditation
Use self-acceptance affirmations mentioned below (or create your own) to sit still and meditate whenever you doubt yourself or are going through a difficult patch.
- I trust myself to do my best
- I am unique and original and that is a blessing
- I believe in myself
- I can be loved only when I love myself
- I can love others unconditionally only when I love myself unconditionally
- My opinions are worthwhile and valuable
- My approval is good enough for me

Maintaining a Diary
Write down answers to the following self-acceptance questions. Crystallizing your thoughts into words will help you improve your level of self-acceptance and self-love.
- What are the things that I know and believe I deserve? Why?

- What is the meaning of trust to me? How can I trust myself more?
- Can you recall a time when you didn't get what you wanted and, later on, you realized it was for the better? Write that event down.

The Practice of Self-Responsibility

NLP Techniques

Swish technique for altering negative thoughts – The Swish NLP technique is designed to teach your brain to think differently and innovatively to triggers of negativity. By practicing the Swish pattern, you are teaching your brain to use the same old cue but react or respond differently.

Let us take the example of a typical scenario in a teenager's life. You have taken the SAT test, and your scores have turned out average. Now, you've decided to take responsibility for it and you are determined to repeat the test for better scores.

Now, you have prepared for the second round of the SAT. However, you are ridden with self-doubts and fears that are eating into your self-confidence. Take the help of the Swish technique so that you can take responsibility for yourself and redo the test with confidence, and free yourself from needless negative thoughts and fears. The Swish NLP uses four components including:

The unwanted trigger or thought – This is the negative thought. So, in your case the negative thought is the image of you walking in to do the test and finding all the questions difficult to answer.

The unwanted feeling – This is the feeling that the bad feelings evoke. So, whenever you imagine the SAT test that is difficult to solve your stomach churns, your palms get all sweaty, and you are filled with panic.

Replacement thought – You have done a lot of preparation and have also undergone multiple mock tests in which your scores were really great. So, you pick a memory of one such successful test and replace your unwanted trigger or thought with this happy memory. Keep repeating the Swish test until your mind is rewired to eliminate anxieties and fears.

It is important to remember that the Swish technique works only when the fears are unfounded and have no tangible basis. You know you have prepared hard for the second round of the test, and you are ready to take it. However, needless and baseless self-doubts are preventing you from taking the plunge.

So you use the Swish NLP technique to rid yourself of these baseless doubts, take responsibility for your hard work and outcomes, and go with confidence to do the retest.

Affirmations

Building self-esteem is in your hands. Take responsibility for yourself. Use these affirmations for personal responsibility to help you:

- I am taking 100% responsibility for what happened, for what is happening, and for what will happen to my life.
- I am responsible for the way my life turns out
- I am certainly not responsible for how others choose to perceive me
- I am responsible for all actions, thoughts, feelings, and

words that I experience and use

- I will honor my commitment to becoming self-responsible, even when I don't like the outcomes

Visualization

Visualization is a powerful tool to use to imagine your future life, and then work to make it a reality. Here is a little exercise you can follow to visualize your future life and take responsibility for achieving it:

- First, sit in a calm and relaxed manner.
- Next, close your eyes and imagine what you see yourself as when you step out of your adolescence.
- What do you see in your mind? The gates of a college? The scene of a graduation day when you are walking up to the stage to receive a prize even as you hear thunderous applause for you in the background?
- Don't entertain any doubts at this stage. Fill in all the details of the imagery; the colors, the smells, the sounds, the people who you want to be with you in the future, and every other important detail. Engrave this image into your mind.
- Now, open your eyes and revel in the joy of achieving your dreams in your mind.
- Take responsibility for this visualization, and begin working to make it a reality.

Meditation

Look at the following example: You are doing a stretching asana in a yoga class. Now, your teacher comes close and presses you to stretch a little harder. You are distracted at that moment. However, following his or her instructions you stretch a little more and pull a muscle. Now, whose fault is it?

Yes, you could blame the teacher for being inexperienced and giving you instructions without knowing your body well. However, if you blame your teacher you become powerless to do anything productive in the future because you have passed on the power to your teacher.

Instead, if you took responsibility for what happened and included factors such as;
- Your own distraction
- Your thoughtless action to follow the teacher's instructions
- Acting impulsively
- Ignoring the first couple of minutes of discomfort you got when you stretched more than you should have done

Meditate on the entire episode, and take responsibility for those things that you could've done right to prevent the muscle tear. This way you empower yourself to take control of your life, and not let someone else sit in the driver's seat.

Maintaining a Diary
Make entries in your diary for all the elements of the day that you disliked. Against each of those elements, make a note of at least two things you could have done or not done which could have altered the outcome favorably for you. Make this a practice, and with each passing day, you will notice your ability to take responsibility for your life improving significantly.

The Practice of Self-Assertiveness

NLP Techniques
One of the most important NLP lessons for self-assertiveness is to learn to say no to people. Do you have friends in your class or

neighborhood who take you for granted? Can you recall how many times you have agreed to do the class bully's homework simply to remain in his or her good books, despite knowing you should have said no?

What about wanting to be picked for the school basketball, football, or cheerleading team? In order to be chosen, have you done favors to people who hold powerful positions? All these are classic examples of lack of self-assertiveness during teenage life. It is important to be conscious of these elements and learn the art of saying no when you are being taken for granted or simply to win a favor.

Instead, build your skills and confidence so that you can assert yourself when the situation calls for it. NLP training involves deconstructing and formulating scenarios, assertive responses, and processes that can be used in a real-life situation. Practice assertive responses and reactions when alone and use them confidently when the need arises. The more you practice these scenarios and enactments, the easier it will be for you to use them in real-life situations.

Affirmations

Repeating these affirmations helps in developing a natural sense of assertiveness to express yourself and your thoughts honestly. These affirmations help you to stand up for your beliefs and values, take control when needed, and speak your mind openly and freely.

- I speak my mind without fear
- I am an assertive person
- I do not hesitate to tell others how I feel
- I am confident when talking to people
- I stand firm when needed

- I stand up for my values and principles
- I confidently control a situation if required
- I do not hesitate to express myself honestly
- Assertiveness is a natural trait in me
- I set clear boundaries when required
- Others respect me because I am self-assertive

Visualization

Suppose you had to give a speech in front of the class. It is on a topic that you are really good at, and there is no reason for panic. Yet your lack of self-assertive skills drives you into a panic mode. What do you do? First, ensure you are thoroughly prepared with your speech. Practice the speech multiple times to make sure there are no errors.

Now, sit in a relaxed manner in a chair and close your eyes. Transport yourself in your mind to your class. Imagine all your classmates sitting in their respective places waiting for you to walk up and give your speech. Now, visualize yourself walking up confidently with your head held high. Imagine yourself standing on the dais, getting ready to give your speech. Imagine smiling confidently.

Repeat the speech in your mind without a mistake. Visualize the confident throw of your voice as you present your ideas. When you finish the speech, visualize getting a great round of applause from your classmates as well as from your teacher. Open your eyes, and feel the confidence of the visualization you just had course through your entire body.

Meditation

Some people mistakenly believe that practicing meditation takes the 'edge off' of self-assertiveness, as you are supported by a mellowed-down attitude brought on by meditation. Nothing can be farther from the truth. Meditation does not make anyone less assertive. On the contrary, it empowers you to handle all situations with lowered levels of stress thereby helping you achieve what you want easily.

Moreover, meditation helps you discern between assertiveness and aggression. It helps you become self-aware thereby giving you the power to articulate your thoughts correctly and in line with your values and principles. Meditate for 15 minutes before you leave for class each day. You can use one of the affirmations like a mantra during your meditation.

Maintaining a Diary
Write down the problems that you faced each day. Next to each of these problems, write down your affirmations. Write down your visualizations for a more successful outcome than you had on that day.

For example, suppose your worst problem at school one day was to be bullied mercilessly. You felt so miserable at being bullied that the tears of self-pity came naturally, which only increased the bullying. The day finally finished.

Now, write down the three most suitable affirmations for the bullying problem you faced today. Examples could be:

- Bullies cannot undermine my power. Their actions only reflect their own lack of confidence.
- Crying while being mercilessly bullied was not a sign of weakness. It was only a natural response to mental pain. There is nothing to be ashamed about.
- I am proud that I did not hit back or behave aggressively with them.

Now, visualize a similar scenario and imagine yourself coming through the unpleasant episode by standing up for yourself, and telling the bullies sternly and firmly to back off. Reading your thoughts will help you build your self-assertiveness.

The Practice of Living with Purpose

NLP Techniques
A powerful NLP tool for living a purposeful life is to set SMART goals. SMART stands for:

S – Specific goals that are clearly stated; for example, 'I will lose 5 pounds by the end of this quarter' is a specific goal, rather than 'I will lose weight.'

M – Measurable goals mean you can determine easily if you have achieved your goals. So, in the above example 5 pounds can be easily measured whereas the second example does not have any measurable aspect to it, and therefore does not constitute a SMART goal.

A – Achievable goals are those that are possible to be achieved. For example, 'I will study to get a GPA score of 4 or above in order to get into a good college' is an achievable goal, especially if your score until now has been hovering around 3. However, 'I will become the next President of the United States' is not achievable, at least not at this stage in your life.

R – Realistic goals means the goals should be achievable after taking into consideration your current circumstances. For example, if your current GPA is hovering between 1.5 and 2, then setting a goal of 4 within the same semester looks unrealistic. You will have to set goals that increase your GPA scores in stages; first try to achieve a 2.5, then a 3, then a 3.5, and finally to 4 and above.

T – Time-bound means your goals must have an expiry date. For example, 'I will achieve a GPA score of 4' is not timebound whereas 'I will achieve a GPA score of 4 by the 3rd semester of college' is timebound

Affirmations

Here are some examples of affirmations for living with a purpose:

- I am connected with my destiny
- I am aligned with the higher purpose of my life
- I can hear my inner voice telling me where to go
- I live a life of passion and purpose
- I dream and then I work to make my dreams a reality
- I create my own life

Visualization

The following visualizations of your life purpose are highly suited for any adolescent. Feel free to choose one of them or dig deeper into your mind to identify and visualize your own destiny.

- Imagine your graduation day on which your family and friends are proudly watching you walk up to the stage to receive the best student award
- Visualize yourself participating in a national or international meet of your favorite game, and winning the gold medal
- Imagine yourself with a hefty bank balance, with a beautiful home, and a loving family
- Imagine yourself traveling the world and becoming a famous travel-blogger
- Visualize yourself driving a snazzy car of your choice

Powerful visualizations enhance your willpower and resolve to help you achieve your life purpose.

Meditation

One of the biggest challenges of living with purpose is that the set purpose is forgotten or lost in the din and noise of everyday living. Your daily school grinds, your social circle times, your tests, assignments, partying, and more - such daily activities take up so much of your time and energy that it is very easy to forget what your purpose of life is.

It is, therefore, imperative that you keep reminding yourself of your life goals. Before retiring to bed or as soon as you wake up in the morning, sit for a couple of minutes in silence and solitude and meditate on your life goal. For example, when the alarm rings to wake you up in the morning don't get off the bed immediately. Sit on it, close your eyes, and repeat to yourself your life goal - whatever it may be:

- I promise I will get into a good college to do my computer science engineering
- Five years from now, I see myself working in one of the best law firms as an intern
- Two years from now, I see myself winning a medal at the national level athletics meet

Maintaining a Diary
The SMART goals are best recorded in your diary along with space to update successful and failed milestones. It is important to keep track of your 'life purpose' diary and ensure all entries are made honestly and objectively. Maintaining a diary helps you reflect on your successes and failures.

Moreover, maintaining a diary helps you remain grounded right through your life. How is this possible? Every time you feel discouraged and depressed, take a peek into your diary and read your success stories and get back that feeling of motivation. Every time you feel overconfident and arrogant about your achievements, read your stories of failure to remind yourself that failure is part and parcel of life. You will learn to be grateful for your successes as well as for the lessons from your failures.

The Practice of Personal Integrity

NLP Techniques
Personal integrity is nothing but walking the talk and talking the walk. You do as you say, and you say only what you do. Therefore, practicing a life of personal integrity calls for a deep level of self-awareness because only when you are aware of your values and principles can you live your life aligned with them. Here are some NLP-based suggestions to practice personal integrity:

- Find the courage to say NO so that you make only those promises that you can keep.
- Learn to be more self-disciplined so that you spend more time doing useful (and promised) things than wasting time in lazing around, attending far more social events than you should, etc.
- Break large jobs into smaller tasks so that it is easy to monitor them and ensure the final promised task is completed on time.

Affirmations
Use the following affirmations to align your heart, mind, and body with your core values and beliefs:

- Everything I say or do is a sincere promise
- I value honesty and integrity above all else
- I practice what I preach
- I do not hesitate to admit my mistakes
- I always do what I believe is right even in the face of

dissension and unpopularity
- I promise only when I can keep it

Visualization
Always imagine keeping promises and seeing the happy faces of the people to whom you have kept your promise. For example, suppose you have promised your friend that you will go to her house to help her complete her science project. Now, suddenly, you have received a party invitation from another set of friends. You can go because you have nothing pending to be done. However, you have given your promise to your friend. The choice you make now reflects your personal integrity. Think and then choose.

Meditation
The more we know and appreciate ourselves, the more we get rooted in personal integrity. As you meditate each day and get in touch with the deep parts of your mind, you understand why you are the way you are. This knowledge will help you stay grounded to your core values which, in turn, help you lead an honest and straightforward life with little or no guile.

Moreover, meditation clears your mind of useless thoughts that only confuse and addle you. A clear and calm mind is the cornerstone of personal integrity. You know where you stand and you know what you need to do to remain there.

Maintaining a Diary
Despite our best efforts, there are times when we end up breaking promises. In the above example wherein you had to choose between going to a fun party and helping your friend, it is possible that you chose to break your promise because the lure of the party was too good to resist.

Remember to make a note of such instances in your diary. Don't forget to add the look of pain that came over your friend's face when you made up a lame excuse the next day, or when she found out that you chose the party over your promise.

The next time such a situation comes up again do go back to read what you have written, and hopefully, that will help you improve your personal integrity. The more you face up to your mistakes, the closer you get to becoming an honest and upright person.

Chapter 5:

Workbook

This questionnaire or workbook is based on the format of the six components as explained in Chapter 4. You need to invest your time and effort to complete the workbook to be able to slowly but surely build the six components of self-esteem in your life. The workbook is general in nature and is flexible enough to fit into any teenager's life.

Complete the quizzes given in Chapter 2 under the six components of self-esteem. Based on the result, arrange the components in increasing order of importance starting from the one that needs your immediate attention (because you rate yourself the lowest in that) and ending with the one that needs your least attention (because you rate yourself highly on that).

Complete the workbooks in the same order as your customized ranking list. For example, if your biggest concern is to find a purpose in life then do the workbook for that first. If your least concern is to live life with personal integrity, then keep the workbook concerned with that component last.

Workbook for the Practice of Living Consciously

NLP techniques – Paying Attention to Your Thoughts
Before going to bed, write down the three most important thoughts that took hold of your mind today:

1)

_____

_____

_____

_____

_____

_____

2)

_____

_____

_____

_____

_____

_____

3)

_____

_____

_____

_____

_____

_____

NLP Techniques – Prayers
On every Sunday night, write down the three most important prayers that you want answered in the coming week:

1)

_____

_____

_____

_____

_____

_____

2)

_____

_____

_____

_____

_____

3)

_____

_____

_____

_____

_____

Affirmations – Write down the three most important affirmations that are aligned with your efforts to live life more consciously than before:

1)

_____

_____

2)_____

_____

3)_____

_____

Visualization – Visualize one goal in your life, and write it down in great detail including:

The scene

_____

The people in it

_____

Smells

_____

Sounds

_____

Your feelings

_____

Meditation – After your meditation session, write down the two most important things that occupied your mind despite your best efforts in trying to keep your focus on meditating:

1)

_____
_____
_____
_____
_____
_____

2)

_____
_____
_____
_____
_____

Maintaining a Diary – At the end of each week, read through your diary and identify one element that recurred at least twice for which you had to show gratitude. If there are more, do make a note of them too;

1)

_____

_____

_____

_____

_____

_____

Workbook for the Practice of Self-Acceptance

NLP Anchoring Technique - Take two of the happiest memories of your life until now, and create anchoring techniques for them so that you have them ready to use whenever needed.

1)

_____

_____

_____

_____

_____

_____

2)

_____

_____

_____

_____

_____

_____

Affirmations – Write down three affirmations for self-acceptance. Think and make your own. Don't copy from what is given in this book:

1)

_____

2)

_____

3)

_____

Visualization – Write down a detailed description of your happy self. What are the things that make you happy and loved?

_____

_____

_____

_____

_____

_____

Meditation – Focus and meditate on any of the following affirmations for self-acceptance or create and use your own:
I love myself the way I am
I accept my strengths with joy and my weaknesses with humility

Workbook for the Practice of Self-Responsibility

The NLP Swish Technique – Write down three unwanted triggers and the corresponding replacement triggers for each of them:

Unwanted   trigger   1)
_____

Replacement   trigger   1)
_____

Unwanted   trigger   2)
_____

Replacement   trigger   2)
_____

Unwanted   trigger   3)
_____

Replacement   trigger   3)
_____

Affirmation – Which of the following self-responsibility affirmations suit you best?
- I take full responsibility for my life.
- I am responsible for whatever happens in my life.
- I honor all commitments in my life, unmindful of deterring obstacles.

Visualization – Write down your most important goal in life, and visualize the day you will achieve it. Write down detailed descriptions of your imagination.

_____
_____
_____

_____
_____
_____

Meditation – Take an example of an event in your life that resulted in pain for you. Think objectively and write down all the contributing factors of the pain. Categorize the factors under two headings:

Under your control

_____
_____
_____
_____
_____

Not under your control

_____
_____
_____
_____
_____

You can use your diary to hunt for such painful situations.

Workbook for the Practice of Self-Assertiveness

NLP Techniques – Look at the following examples and answer honestly:

If you had to choose between staying back to complete your assignment and going for a great party, which would you choose and why?

If you had to choose between a friend who is boring but a topper in class and a friend who is great fun to be with but can lead you astray, who will you choose as your best friend?

Practice answers to these questions so that when a real-life situation comes, your mind is ready to make the appropriate choice backed by sound reasoning.

Affirmations – Complete the following affirmations for self-assertiveness in your own words:

1) I am _____

2) I am not deterred by _____

3) I stand up for _____

Visualization – Think of a situation in your life that keeps repeating in which you find it extremely difficult to say no. Now, visualize the same event in your mind and imagine saying no. Write down the details of your imagination; your words, gestures, body language, tone of voice, etc.

_____

_____

_____

_____

_____

_____

Workbook for the Practice of Living with Purpose

NLP Techniques – Write down your goals and ensure they are fulfilling the SMART technique:

- S – Specific

- M – Measurable
- A – Achievable
- R -Realistic
- T – Timebound

Affirmations – Write down three affirmations that are most suited for your purpose in life:

1)

_____

_____

2)

_____

_____

3)

_____

_____

Visualization – Rate the following goals in order of the importance in your life:

- Graduating from college
- Getting a medal in an important sports event
- Being financially successful in life
- Traveling the world
- Becoming a successful musician

Now, for the first two goals visualize a successful end result and write them down in detail. If none of the above-mentioned goals are in your list, then go ahead and make your own choices.

Workbook for the Practice of Personal Integrity

NLP Techniques – Look at the following examples of how to say no politely, and rank them in the order of your preference from the most liked to the least liked. Then practice using them, and don't forget to say no when you are sure you cannot keep promises:
- This is not a good fit for me
- Sounds interesting, but right now I'm really pressed for time
- I am afraid I'll have to pass up your invitation this time
- If I agreed to help you, I will be forced to break my promise
- Sorry, this doesn't fit my schedule

Affirmations – Write down three affirmations that are most suitable for your lifestyle:

1)

_____

_____

2)

_____

_____

3)

_____

_____

Maintaining a Diary – Think of two of the most embarrassing times in your life when you did not keep your promises. Now, answer the following questions based on those experiences:

What were reasons for you to break the promise?

_____

_____

_____

_____

What were your feelings?

_____

_____

_____

_____

What lessons have you learned from those experiences which helped you grow your personal integrity?

_____

_____

_____

_____

Chapter 6:

Conclusion

The most crucial lesson in your journey of building and developing self-esteem is the fact that it is a never-ending journey. You can never reach a situation where you can say that you have nothing more to do in terms of building your self-esteem. Each stage in your life will bring new challenges which could affect your self-esteem, and you might need to start again from scratch.

You have to continuously upgrade your knowledge and skills regarding the basic components of self-esteem that are discussed in this book including:

- Living consciously
- Self-acceptance
- Self-responsibility
- Self-assertiveness
- Living with purpose
- Personal integrity

As you grow from a teenager into an adult and face the challenges of the wide world outside, you will be grateful for having become aware of the importance of self-esteem and its components early on in life. Not many people are fortunate enough to have got the insight to develop this crucial personality trait from the age of adolescence.

The habits learned and mastered during your adolescence will get so deeply embedded in your psyche that they will always be part of your system. So, picking up good habits during your teenage days is the best way to keep them in your long-term memory.

So, go ahead and start your journey of self-discovery to build and develop your self-esteem. Be prepared to keep learning and moving forward.

Made in the USA
San Bernardino, CA
30 January 2019